KNOWLEDGE ENCYCLOPEDIA
ASTRONOMY
SPACE

(An imprint of Prakash Books Pvt. Ltd.)

Wonder House Books
Corporate & Editorial Office
113-A, 1st Floor, Ansari Road,
Daryaganj, New Delhi-110002
Tel +91 11 2324 7062-65

Disclaimer: The information contained in this encyclopedia has been collated with inputs from subject experts. All information contained herein is true to the best of the Publisher's knowledge.

Printed in 2020 in India

ISBN : 9789390391585

Table of Contents

AMAZING **ASTRONOMY**

"Man must rise above Earth—to the top of the atmosphere and beyond—
for only thus will he fully understand the world in which he lives."
—**Socrates**

Astronomy is one of the oldest sciences in the world. It includes the study of all objects and phenomena that are outside Earth's atmosphere (i.e. they are extra-terrestrial). These objects have been studied for thousands of years by people called astronomers. This ancient science dates back to the Babylonians and other early recorded civilisations, who, even at that time, recognised some of the constellations we see today. With the observance of regular astronomical events, charts and calendars were created, for the purpose of **astrology**, to predict seasons and keep track of the passage of time. New ideas were introduced by Greek philosophers like Pythagoras about the shape of Earth and the motion of objects in the universe. Greek astronomers like Ptolemy supported the theory of Earth being at the centre of the universe (a geocentric universe). The 17th century was when the telescope was invented, and the laws of motion and gravity were discovered.

Astronomy has been used over the centuries for the purpose of navigation. Though astrology was earlier associated with astronomy, since the former lacks a scientific basis, the two are no longer connected.

Today, with advances in science and technology, the scope of the observational science of astronomy has expanded considerably and includes not only the study of the solar system but also objects and events from way, way beyond.

▼ *An astronaut's window to the marvels of the universe*

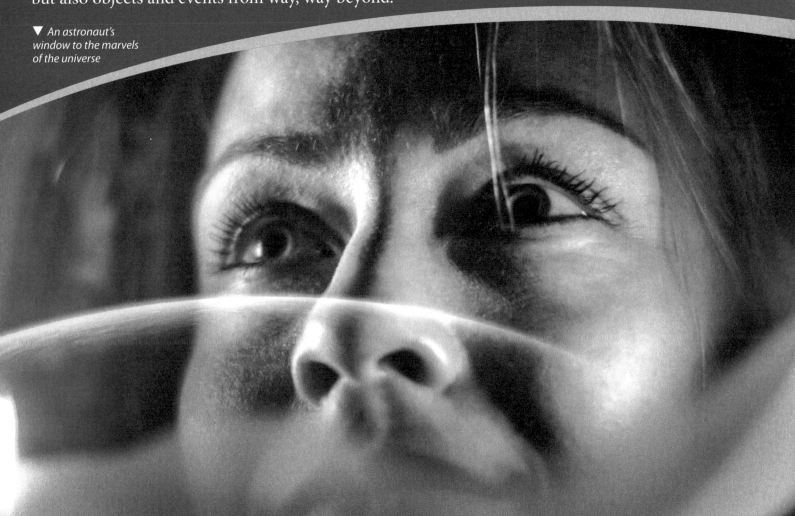

A Brief History

Astronomy was one of the first few natural sciences to develop. However, unlike other such sciences, it had reached a high level of refinement and achievement by the second half of the first millennium BCE. It has been one of the most enduring traditions across the world for almost 4000 years.

⭐ Astronomy in Ancient Times

The Nebra Sky Disc is the oldest known representation of the cosmos. It is the earliest record of astronomical observations depicting the Sun, a lunar crescent and stars. In the Bronze Age, this was a kind of astronomical clock or tool used in agriculture for finding out the correct time for sowing and harvesting. The 1600 BCE bronze tool has a diameter of 32 centimetres and weighs approximately 2 kilograms.

Early recordings of astronomical phenomena are also found in the ancient Babylonian, Chinese, Central American and North European cultures. These ancient cultures tried to measure time; trace the movements of the Sun, the Moon and the stars; track the regularity in the occurrence of sunrises, sunsets and other celestial events through structures they built. The rock formation of Stonehenge in the UK is evidence of this. Native Americans also left behind rock drawings (petroglyphs) of astronomical phenomena.

▲ *The Nebra Sky Disc was discovered in 1999 in Germany, by treasure hunters using a metal detector. It depicts the Sun or a full Moon, stars and a crescent Moon*

▲ Stonehenge

⭐ Timeline of Astronomy

The history of astronomy is long and spread across many nations. Many cultures learned from each other to make advances in this field.

Ancient Mayans note the 18.6-year cycle of Earth's Moon rising and setting. They prepare a calendar charting the movements of the planets, the Moon and the Sun.

750 BCE

▶ *A Mayan astronomer is depicted within the pages of the Madrid Codex, a Mayan book about almanacs and horoscopes*

585-470 BCE

Ancient Greeks build on the knowledge of the Mayans to predict eclipses. Specifically, Thales uses this knowledge and predicts a solar eclipse. A Greek philosopher named Anaxagoras provides an accurate explanation of eclipses. He describes the Sun and how the Moon reflects light from the Sun.

▶ *Anaxagoras also tried to explain the occurrence of meteors and rainbows. He described the Sun as a large, fiery mass*

400 BCE

The ancient Babylonians learn to record the position of celestial bodies by dividing the heavens into twelve 30-degree segments under the Zodiac system.

387 BCE

A famous Greek philosopher named Plato starts a school called the Academy. Plato proposes that planets follow perfectly circular orbits and that all celestial bodies move around Earth.

► A part of a much larger fresco depicting the School of Athens; Plato and Aristotle are depicted here

350 BCE

Aristotle, another well-known Greek philosopher and scientist, plays a key role in the development of Western thought. He publishes *On the Heavens,* which is the oldest existing source clearly mentioning that Earth is a sphere and gives valid reasons to support his claim. He arrives at this conclusion by observing Earth's circular shadow on the Moon during a lunar eclipse.

◄ Aristotle wrote a book called On the Heavens, based on his observations of the universe

330 BCE

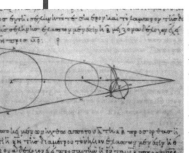

Greek astronomer Aristarchus of Samos proposes a system where the Sun is the central figure around which Earth and the other planets move. This is called the **heliocentric model** of the solar system. This leads to the geocentric versus heliocentric debate.

▲ A Greek copy of Aristarchus's notes on the relative sizes of the Sun, Earth and the Moon

270 BCE

Heraclides, a Greek philosopher and astronomer and the first to suggest the rotation of Earth, proposes the very first model of our solar system. In this model, he puts the planets in order and places Earth at the very centre of the model. This is the obsolete **geocentric model** of the solar system.

▲ Heraclides was a pupil of Plato

250 BCE

Greek philosophers Eratosthenes (known for the oldest surviving record measuring Earth's size) and Aristarchus use simple geometry to calculate the size of Earth, the Moon and the Sun, as well as the distances between the planets nearby. They estimate the size of the universe relative to Earth.

▲ The illustration depicts Eratosthenes's time as a teacher in Alexandria

100 BCE

Hipparchus, a Greek astronomer and mathematician, prepares the first star catalogue and constructs a celestial globe with the stars and constellations arranged on it.

46 BCE

Julius Caesar introduces the Julian calendar, similar to the one we use today, to the Roman Empire. It is a purely solar calendar and includes leap years.

▲ A bust of Julius Caesar

⭐ Incredible Individuals

While working on the Julian calendar, the Alexandrian astronomer Sosigenes miscalculated the length of the year by 11 minutes and 14 seconds. Over the centuries, this seemingly minor mistake had led to a 10-day deviation. So, as a reformative step, Pope Gregory XIII introduced the Gregorian calendar (which we use till date) in 1582.

Renaissance & Astronomy

The Renaissance period (14th–16th century) saw a rebirth of European culture, art, politics, economics and science. This era was also characterised by a heightened interest in the study of everything related to ancient Greece and Rome, and the discovery of new territories and continents. Astronomy too played a key role as important advances in science were made and new theories about the universe were put forth by astronomers. Great artists, scientists, thinkers, authors and statesmen flourished during this time.

⭐ Nicolaus Copernicus (1473–1543)

Although Copernicus, the father of modern astronomy, wasn't the first to challenge Ptolemy's geocentric theory, he reinvented the heliocentric model. He was the first person to publish his claim, thereby challenging the doctrine of the Church.

Copernicus concluded that Earth and all the planets in the solar system revolve around the Sun. He also proposed that Earth rotates daily on its axis, and what human beings see in the night skies depends on Earth's motion. Copernicus did not have the equipment to validate his theories, and he was proved correct much later in the 1600s by astronomers like Galileo Galilei.

▲ *An oil painting by Jan Matejko depicts Nicolaus Copernicus looking at the skies from the balcony of a cathedral. It is titled 'Conversations with God'*

💡 Isn't It Amazing!

It is indeed amazing that Copernicus made many of his astronomical observations with the naked eye! He passed away more than 50 years before Galileo Galilei first observed the skies using a telescope he had made.

▲ *An illustration of Tycho Brahe*

⭐ Tycho Brahe (1546–1601)

Danish astronomer Tycho Brahe was the first 'true' observer of the skies—he built the Danish Observatory using **sextants** instead of a telescope (which had not yet been invented). A sextant is an instrument used to determine the angle between the horizon and a celestial object like a star, the Sun or the Moon. He showed that the Sun was much farther than the Moon from Earth by using **trigonometry**, a branch of mathematics concerned with functions of angles and their application to calculations.

⭐ Johannes Kepler (1571–1630)

A German astronomer named Johannes Kepler supported Copernicus's heliocentric model in his book, *The Cosmographic Mystery*. He became one of the first figures in the field of astronomy to offer public support to the theories proposed by Copernicus.

Kepler was a student of Tycho Brahe. The two worked together briefly before Brahe's death in 1601. Brahe's database and his observation of an exploding star (a supernova) made Kepler realise that planets and other bodies moved in ellipses. This became his first law of planetary motion out of the three. Till his discovery, it was believed that planets travelled in a circular path instead of an oval path.

▶ *The painting depicts Johannes Kepler holding a protractor. He was a mathematician and an optician*

✪ Galileo Galilei (1564–1642)

Italian scientist Galileo Galilei was the pioneer of modern 'observational' astronomy. In the early 1600s, he made path-breaking discoveries using extremely powerful telescopes made by him, which were based on a model invented in the Netherlands around the time. Based on his observations of Venus, he accepted and explained the heliocentric model of the universe. This went against the prevalent theory of the geocentric system.

▲ *Galilei shows the chief magistrate of Venice how to use a telescope*

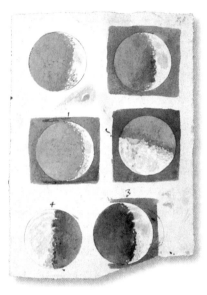

▲ *Galilei drew the Moon's phases and discovered that it had an uneven surface using a powerful telescope magnified up to 20 times*

Galilei made groundbreaking astronomical discoveries that went against the assumptions made by people before him. For example, while many believed that the Moon's surface is smooth, he rightly claimed it to be uneven. Galilei also made observations about the puzzling appearance of Saturn and its atmosphere, which later turned out to be its rings, and also explained the nature of sunspots. He claimed that Venus goes through phases like Earth's Moon and was also responsible for the discovery of four of Jupiter's moons.

The latter two observations implied that there existed more than one centres of motion in the cosmos and that the planets revolved around the Sun. It was a decisive moment in the world of science and astronomy.

These discoveries went against the belief of the Roman Catholic Church, which believed that Earth was the central body in the solar system. So, Galilei was sentenced to life imprisonment. He died due to an illness while under house arrest.

▲ *A painting of Galilei*

▼ *Galilei facing the Roman Catholic Church during an inquisition*

Modern Astronomy

The period between the 18th and 20th centuries was marked by the discovery of the outer planets of the solar system as well as discoveries in stellar and galactic areas. From the late 19th century onwards, astronomy also included **astrophysics**. While astronomy is the science that measures the positions and characteristics of heavenly bodies, the application of the laws and theories of physics to understand astronomy is called astrophysics. Scientists also researched gases and dust particles found close to and in between the stars, and nuclear reactions that provide the energy radiated by stars. Cosmology—the study of the origins of the universe—was another area of interest and focus in this period.

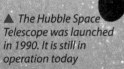

▲ The Hubble Space Telescope was launched in 1990. It is still in operation today

▲ An illustration of Cassini

▲ Sir Isaac Newton examining the nature of light

★ Gian Domenico Cassini (1625–1712)

Italian-born French astronomer, Gian Domenico Cassini, amongst others, discovered a dark gap—the Cassini Division—between the A and B rings of Saturn, in 1675. He also discovered four moons of Saturn—Lapetus, Rhea, Tethys and Dione. He mainly studied the Sun, but later with the use of powerful telescopes, he also studied the planets. He was the first to notice the shadows cast by Jupiter's moons as they travelled between Jupiter and the Sun. He measured its rotational period after observing the spots on its surface and discovered the flattened poles of Jupiter and the zodiacal light. Although Cassini did not easily accept new ideas and theories, he is still remembered as one of the important astronomers of the 17th and 18th centuries.

★ Sir Isaac Newton (1643–1727)

English physicist and mathematician, Sir Isaac Newton is one of the greatest scientists in history. Newton developed the three laws of motion (which became the foundation for physics), the theory of gravity and a new branch of mathematics called calculus. He also advanced the science of optics, contributing significantly towards reflecting telescopes; worked on **diffraction**; and came up with the theory of light.

👤✓ In Real Life

Despite astronomy having developed into an advanced science, one of its major pitfalls is that it is an 'observational' science rather than one based on scientific experiments. A majority of the measurements have to be undertaken at great distances from the objects being studied, without any control over their temperature, pressure or chemical composition. The only exceptions being meteorites (pieces of asteroids which land on Earth); lunar surface soil and rock samples; comet and asteroid dust samples brought back by robotic spacecrafts; and interplanetary dust particles in and above the stratosphere—which can be tested in a laboratory environment.

▲ Edmond Halley

▲ Pierre-Simon, marquis de Laplace

▲ Joseph-Louis Lagrange

⭐ Edmond Halley (1656–1742)

An English mathematician and astronomer, Edmond Halley was the first to calculate the orbit of a comet. He also played a key role in the publication of Newton's *Mathematical Principles of Natural Philosophy*.

In 1678, he published a star catalogue comprising locations of southern stars determined using a telescope. The first work of its type to be published, it helped establish him as a reputed astronomer.

⭐ Pierre-Simon, marquis de Laplace (1749–1827)

French mathematician, astronomer and physicist, Laplace was known for his contributions in exploring the stability of the solar system. Some observed that there are disturbances in the solar system which are caused by the fact that all planets are attracted by the Sun. However, they are also attracted—though by a smaller degree—by all the other planets. New mathematical methodology was developed in the 18th century to provide a more efficient rationale for such disturbances. Laplace and Joseph-Louis Lagrange (1736–1813) played an important role in showing that the solar system was actually quite stable.

Rockets: Raring to Rise!

What is a rocket? It is a **propulsion** device which carries solid or liquid **propellants** and provides both the fuel and the **oxidiser** needed for combustion, independent of the atmosphere. Rockets are an integral part of space exploration today; they help carry spacecrafts to other planets, satellites into space and supplies to the International Space Station. Let us find out how rockets originated.

▲ *A bust of the Greek Archytas who first flew a wooden pigeon*

⭐ Early 'Rockets'

One of the first objects to be successfully flown using rocket flight principles was a wooden bird. It might have been shaped like a pigeon. It was flown by a Greek named Archytas in 400 BCE. The bird was suspended on wires and pushed upwards by escaping steam. Archytas used the action-reaction principle to fly his wooden bird. This principle was recognised as a scientific law only in the 17th century.

300 years later, Hero, another Greek from Alexandria, developed a device called an aeolipile, which used rocket propulsion principles. It was shaped like a sphere and had L-shaped tubes on two sides. It was kept above a kettle of boiling water. When the water turned into steam, it moved upwards and entered the two tubes, causing the sphere to rotate.

▲ *A modern version of Hero's aeolipile*

⭐ Rocket-like Inventions

Exactly when the first real rockets were built is unclear. The Chinese experimented with tubes filled with gunpowder and discovered that the tubes could be launched by escaping gas. In 1232, they used 'arrows of flying fire'—a simple form of a solid-propellant rocket—to scare Mongol invaders. After the war, even the Mongols began making rockets, and this technique may possibly have spread to Europe.

Johann Schmidlap, a 16th-century German firecracker manufacturer, invented a multistaged vehicle to propel fireworks to greater heights. A large skyrocket carried a smaller skyrocket. Once the larger rocket burned up, the smaller one carried on going higher until it burned up too. This is the fundamental principle behind current space rockets.

▶ *A Soyuz rocket being launched*

The Science of Developing Rockets

In the late 17th century, Sir Isaac Newton laid the foundations of modern scientific rocketry through his three laws of motion. His laws explain the how and why of rocketry and outline the reasons why rockets work in the vacuum of outer space. The French and the Dutch were both using rockets for military operations and by 1668, military rockets grew in terms of size and performance. In the same year, a German colonel designed a 60-kilogram rocket. However, the use of rockets in military campaigns declined over the next 100 years.

▲ *A scene from the Anglo-Mysore War where Tipu Sultan's army used rocket artillery against the British*

Then, in the late 18th century, Hyder Ali, prince of Mysore, improved rockets by using metal cylinders instead of paper to contain the burning powder. This was an important development. The range of such rockets was more than a kilometre and they were particularly effective against cavalry. Hyder Ali's son, Tipu Sultan continued to effectively increase the use of rockets against the British in the battles that took place in 1792 and 1799. This inspired Colonel William Congreve to develop extremely successful rocket weapons for the British military. However, improved artillery lead to a decline in the use of rockets in war.

The three pioneers of modern rocketry and space exploration were Russian scientist Konstantin Tsiolkovsky (1857–1935), American professor and inventor Dr. Robert Goddard (1882–1945) and German scientist Hermann Oberth (1894–1989).

▲ *A portrait of Colonel William Congreve*

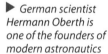

◀ *A photograph of the Russian rocket scientist Konstantin Tsiolkovsky*

▶ *German scientist Hermann Oberth is one of the founders of modern astronautics*

Working Principle

Rockets use liquid or solid fuels. According to Newton's third law of motion, for every action or force, there is an equal and opposite reaction. As per this law, a rocket engine produces a driving force through action and reaction. The engine burns fuel, producing hot gases which flow in one direction and propel the rocket with force in the opposite direction.

ⓥ Incredible Individuals

American professor and inventor, Dr. Robert Goddard earned his doctorate from Clark University in Worcester, where he also taught physics and carried out rocket experiments. Amongst other things, he was the first to develop a rocket motor using liquid fuels, which was used in German V-2 rocket weapons nearly 15 years later. His well-known work, *A Method of Reaching Extreme Altitudes* was published in 1919.

◀ *A photograph of Robert Goddard. NASA's Goddard Space Flight Centre is named after him*

▶ *Goddard standing next to his first rocket*

A Brief History of Telescopes

The telescope was an important invention of the 17th century. It helped astronomers get a closer look at the heavenly bodies. It also helped in getting the scientific and religious communities to accept the heliocentric model of the solar system, which placed the Sun at the centre. The invention of the telescope revolutionised space exploration like never before.

⭐ The First Telescope

Hans Lipperhey from the Netherlands made a patent application in October 1608, for a device which made distant objects appear as if they were close by—the earliest known record of a telescope. The instrument had a positive and negative lens at opposing ends of a thin tube. Galileo Galilei heard about this invention and went ahead and made his own.

▶ *Hans Lipperhey applied for a patent for his invention but was refused*

⭐ Using Telescopes

In 1609, Galilei became the first person to use the telescope to view celestial bodies. However, some others have claimed to use a telescope for this purpose before him. Despite the fact that the early telescopes were small and not as powerful as the modern ones, Galilei managed to observe that Earth's Moon had mountains and craters, spotted a ribbon-like pattern of scattered light across the sky (Milky Way galaxy), and discovered four of Jupiter's moons.

⭐ Development of the Telescope

▲ *Seen here is one of Galilei's early telescopes, now kept in a museum in Florence*

Astronomy thrived after bigger and more powerful telescopes were made. Astronomers were able to view many more features of outer space, including faint faraway stars, and also calculate their stellar distances.

Another instrument, the **spectroscope**, helped gain information about the chemical composition and movement of heavenly bodies in the 19th century. In the 20th century, better telescopes enabled viewing objects in the depths of space. However, due to the interference of the atmosphere, the view did not improve any further.

▼ *The European Southern Observatory's Very Large Telescope (VLT) sits on top of a remote mountain in the Atacama Desert in Chile. Seen here in the photograph are two of the four unit telescopes that comprise the VLT, an extremely advanced telescope made using cutting-edge technology. Source: ESO/José Francisco Salgado (josefrancisco.org)*

How do Telescopes Work?

The early telescopes used 'lenses'—curved pieces of clear glass—to focus light. Today, curved mirrors are used in telescopes. Mirrors are lighter and easier to use than lenses, so they can be made perfectly smooth. With mirrors, the image appears upside down, this is easily resolved by using another mirror to flip the image back.

Mirrors or lenses used in the telescope are referred to as 'optics'. These optics need to be really big in a large and powerful telescope, in order to get a better view of faint far-off objects. The telescope is able to concentrate more light with bigger mirrors or lenses—it is this light that we see when we peer into a telescope. Telescopes made using lenses and mirrors are known as refracting and reflecting telescopes respectively.

▲ A telescope on the deck of the Eiffel Tower in Paris, France

Limitations of a Ground Telescope

When celestial bodies are viewed from a ground telescope, irrespective of how powerful the telescope might be, the vision is distorted due to shifting air pockets in Earth's atmosphere. Such atmospheric distortion makes it look like the stars are twinkling. Also, some wavelengths of radiation (ultraviolet, gamma and X-rays) are partially blocked or absorbed by the atmosphere. For scientists, this is a problem since it is best for them to examine a body like a star by studying all the types of emitted wavelengths. The most effective way to circumvent this problem is to position the telescope beyond the atmosphere, in observatories in space like Fermi, Chandra, Kepler, Spitzer and Planck, to name a few.

▲ A modern-day ground telescope

⊙ Incredible Individuals

American astrophysicist Lyman Spitzer (1914–1997) was interested in the physical processes occurring in interstellar space. In 1946, he first proposed the idea of an orbiting space telescope unhindered by Earth's atmosphere. This finally resulted in the building and launch of the Hubble Space Telescope, in 1990, and other such observatories. In 2003, an orbiting infrared observatory called the Spitzer Space Telescope was named after him.

▲ Lyman Spitzer

Analysing Data from Telescopes

There is no single telescope that can look at all elements of space at once.
Today, there are different types of telescopes that are used to observe celestial bodies in outer space and collect varying types of data from them. The reason for this is that space is dynamic. It becomes difficult to get the same image twice or recreate an image taken from a telescope at a later time. Scientists require different telescopes to point to the same object in space to get a full understanding of it.

▲ *An artist's interpretation of a bright gamma-ray burst*

 ## Types of Telescopes

The earliest telescopes were optical telescopes. These can be of two basic types, refractors and reflectors. While a refractor makes use of convex lenses to gather light, reflectors use concave mirrors. Galilei used a refractive telescope to make his discoveries. Sir Isaac Newton invented the first reflecting telescope in 1671. The 'objective' is a part of a telescope that collects light and determines if the telescope is refractive or reflective. Similarly, radio telescopes collect weak radio light waves and focus and amplify them for further analysis.

Telescopes are also built to serve many different purposes. They are accordingly classified into different types. For example, a solar telescope is made to specifically look at the Sun and gather data from it. A telescope that is sent to outer space is called a space telescope. An astronomer might make use of one or more types of telescopes to study space. However, the data collected from them is not synchronised.

▶ *Some novices and non-professionals buy amateur telescopes to make their observations. The pictured telescope is an amateur solar telescope*

 ## Reading a Telescope

All telescopes work according to some basic principles—one being that the telescope relies on the interaction between energy and matter. The atomic matter or material used to make a telescope is carefully chosen so that it can read the energy emitted from a celestial object. This energy is in the form of electromagnetic waves.

The problem is that most objects emit different frequencies of energy at the same time. This is even true for the energy emitted from your body. So, different wavelengths give the observer different data. This is why different telescopes are required to observe different data. Scientists build their telescopes according to the type of data they want to collect.

▶ *Radio telescopes need to be much larger than other telescopes so that they can accurately collect astronomical radio signals, and not lose them due to the noise produced on Earth*

◀ *A reflecting telescope at the McDonald Observatory in Texas*

The Hubble Space Telescope

Hubble Space Telescope It is named after the foremost observational cosmologist of the 20th century, Edwin Hubble. This telescope was designed and built by the European Space Agency and National Aeronautics and Space Administration. It was deployed on April 25, 1990.

▲ *Edwin Hubble*

▲ *The Hubble Space Telescope being deployed into space*

⭐ The Hubble Telescope's Activities

The Hubble Space Telescope has played an important role in:

* Helping estimate the age of the universe, which is believed to be almost 14 billion years old
* Detecting black holes
* Revealing faraway galaxies
* Discovering dark energy—a force causing the universe to expand at a galloping rate
* Capturing strong explosions of energy during the collapse of gigantic stars
* Studying the atmosphere of planets outside the solar system, which revolve around stars.

▲ *More than 1.3 million observations have been made by the Hubble Space Telescope*

⭐ Instruments and Equipment on Hubble

Hubble uses cutting-edge technology and very specialised equipment. For example, its Fine Guidance Sensors—which lock onto stars as Hubble orbits Earth—are part of its Pointing Control System and help Hubble aim precisely in the correct direction. In fact, the telescope has the ability to lock on to a target object located about 1.6 kilometres away by moving no more than the width of a human hair!

Hubble's mirrors collect 40,000 times more light than the human eye. It uses five main scientific instruments including the Wide Field Camera 3 and spectrographs (which split light into its individual wavelengths). The Wide Field Camera 3 can see three types of light—near-ultraviolet, visible and near-infrared. The first and the third types cannot be seen by people.

🏅 Incredible Individuals

German-born British astronomer, Sir William Herschel (1738–1822) started off as a musician. A book on telescope construction got him interested in astronomy. He wanted to observe distant celestial objects, for which he required powerful telescopes with large mirrors to collect sufficient light. He was compelled to make his own mirrors. His contribution to developing the telescope in the 18th century was crucial.

▶ *British astronomer William Herschel was the one to discover the planet Uranus*

💡 Isn't It Amazing!

Hubble does not travel to the stars, planets or galaxies, instead it takes pictures of them as it whirls around Earth at about 37,300 kmph.

More than 15,000 scientific papers have been published using Hubble's data, making it one of the most productive scientific instruments ever built.

The International Space Station

The International Space Station (ISS) is the largest space laboratory in low Earth orbit. It was launched by the USA and Russia along with the help of experts from Europe, Japan and Canada. Brazil and 11 members of the ESA helped in its construction.

 ## The Origins of ISS

President Ronald Reagan had given NASA the go-ahead for this initiative in the 1980s. In the 1990s, it was redesigned to reduce costs. In 1993, USA and Russia decided to combine their individual space station plans and amalgamate their technologies, expertise and modules with contributions from the ESA and Japan.

The construction of the ISS started in November 1998, with the launch of the Russian control module Zarya and the US-built Unity connecting node. They were linked in orbit by American space shuttle astronauts. Thereafter, constant additions were made, including a control centre, complex laboratories, equipment and habitats. The ISS was completely functional by May 2009.

▲ *The International Space Station*

▶ *A photograph of the International Space Station seen from Atlantis STS-135, after undocking in May 2010*

☀ Isn't It Amazing!

Here are some interesting facts about the ISS:
- the crew lives and works on the ISS while travelling at about 8 kmps.
- in 24 hours, ISS orbits Earth 16 times; it witnesses 16 sunrises and sunsets.
- the living and working space of the ISS—which is larger than a six-bedroom house—consists of six sleeping quarters, two bathrooms and even a gym.
- the ISS measures approximately 108 metres end to end, just 91 centimetres less than a full-length American football field.
- more than 50 computers on-board control the systems.

▲ *Destiny Lab module of ISS*

Assembling the ISS

The ISS is one of the greatest multinational collaborations ever attempted. The Russian-built Zvezda, a habitat and control centre, was added to the ISS in mid-2000. Destiny, a microgravity lab designed by NASA was added to conduct experiments. The Columbus lab, Europe's first long-duration crewed space laboratory, was added to conduct experiments in life sciences and other areas, as was the Japanese-made Kibo Laboratory.

Besides the Russian modules, other elements were added over the years. Some were brought to the ISS by space shuttles and assembled by astronauts during a spacewalk, also known as an Extravehicular Activity (EVA), in orbit. Space shuttles and the Soyuz spacecraft served to transport astronauts back and forth. A Soyuz remained there at all times as a rescue vehicle. In 2006, a pair of solar wings and a thermal radiator were added.

The ISS has a 16-metre-long, Canadian-built Canadarm2, which is a large robotic arm that serves as a crane and is used for a variety of tasks. The ISS has six docking ports that allow six spacecrafts to visit the station simultaneously. In November 2000, the ISS welcomed its first resident crew, American astronaut William Shepherd and Russian cosmonauts Sergey Krikalyov and Yuri Gidzenko. Since then, the ISS has been constantly occupied and has had over 200 astronauts from 18 countries visit it.

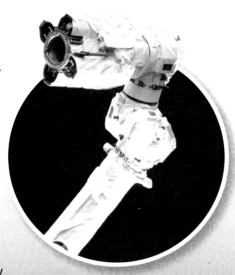

▲ *A part at the end of the robotic arm Canadarm2 used to grip objects and latch onto the station*

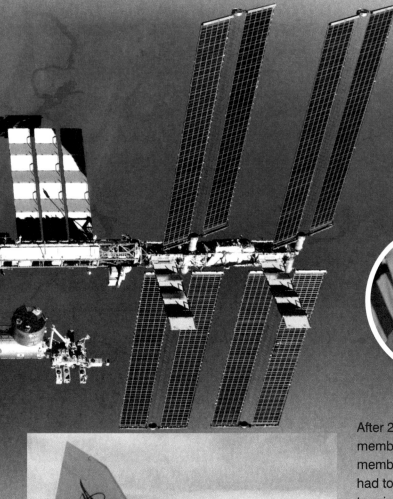

ⓥ Incredible Individuals

American biochemist and astronaut, Peggy Whitson was the first woman commander of the ISS and holds the record for spending the maximum time in space amongst American astronauts. She spent 665 days in space!

◄ *NASA's Peggy Whitson conducted four spacewalks as a member of Expeditions 50, 51 and 52 on the ISS and contributed to hundreds of experiments*

After 2009, the ISS was able to accommodate six crew members (generally three Russians, two Americans and one member from ESA, Japan or Canada). Two Soyuz 'lifeboats' had to be stationed there at all times. In 2011, after the termination of the space shuttle programme, the ISS was serviced by Russia's Progress, Europe's ATV, Japan's H-II Transfer Vehicle and two commercially-run cargo vehicles by SpaceX and Orbital Sciences Corporation. While there is no end date for the ISS mission, in 2014, former President Barack Obama's administration indicated that it would receive support till 'at least 2024'.

▲ *A crew return vehicle of the ISS*

The Space Shuttle

A space shuttle is a partially reusable rocket-launched vehicle. It was designed by NASA to carry astronauts and cargo to and fro spacecrafts in Earth's orbit. It served for 30 years, till July 2011.

⭐ Uses of the Space Shuttle

The space shuttle could carry seven astronauts. During its lifetime, it ferried nearly 355 people to space, launched satellites and functioned as an orbiting science laboratory. The shuttle's crew often repaired other spacecrafts and equipment; the Hubble Space Telescope is an example of this. It went on a few military missions and in later years, was often used for ISS work. Its main parts can be seen in the picture given below.

NASA had five orbiters, of which Columbia and Challenger were lost due to accidents. Discovery, Atlantis and Endeavour are now in museums across the USA. The Enterprise orbiter never went to space, instead it was used for testing.

▼ *Seen here is the Discovery space shuttle before the launch of the STS-114 mission*

— A large external fuel tank

Rocket booster

A pair of long and thin solid rocket boosters to provide thrust to lift off the shuttle on launch

The large white space plane was the orbiter, which went into orbit and was where the crew lived and worked. It comprised a payload bay for transporting cargo

▲ *Seen here is Atlantis—one of the five orbiters of the space shuttle—after it undocked from the International Space Station in September 2006*

⭐ Launching and Landing

Just like a rocket, the space shuttle took off with the help of rocket boosters. These burned for approximately two minutes, were dropped into the ocean, retrieved and reused. The main engines fired for another six minutes. Then the external fuel tank detached and burned up. By this time, the shuttle and crew were in orbit.

On its return, the engines were fired to slow down the craft, and glide it on to a runway for landing. Upon touchdown, a parachute helped lower its speed.

💡 Isn't It Amazing!

The space shuttle's orbiters are humungous and would equal the length of nearly three and a half school buses (each being about 12 metres long)!

▶ *The Space Shuttle Orbiter Pathfinder*

Satellites

An object that moves around a larger object is known as a satellite. There could be a natural satellite like the Moon because it moves around Earth, or an artificial satellite such as a man-made machine. Both types of satellites orbit a larger astronomical body. Generally, natural satellites orbit a planet. Sir Isaac Newton was the first to suggest the idea of an artificial satellite in orbital flight, in 1687. Let us take a look at artificial satellites in Earth's orbit.

▲ A satellite in space orbiting Earth

▶ Earth's Moon is an example of a natural satellite

⭐ Where Do Satellites Orbit?

Artificial satellites like space stations, space shuttle orbiters, etc., can be crewed or unmanned and controlled by robotics. Since the launch of the first artificial satellite, Sputnik 1, over 5,000 satellites have been launched into Earth's orbit by more than 70 different countries. Others have been sent into orbit around Venus, Mars, Jupiter, Saturn, Earth's Moon and also the asteroid Eros.

👤✓ In Real Life

Global environmental changes are a matter of grave concern in the 21st century. These include the effects of global warming, ozone depletion and widespread changes in land cover due to human activities like **biomass burning**. Satellites have proved to be very useful in monitoring these activities on Earth. Satellite pictures enable scientists to 'view' Earth and understand the actual extent and impact of such activities on our planet. Data from satellites helps differentiate between environmental changes caused by human beings versus those caused by nature. NASA's Mission to Planet Earth programme is one such study of Earth from space.

▲ Deforestation has caused the depletion of rainforests in Brazil

⭐ Why are Satellites Important?

Satellites vary greatly in size, design and function. Information about Earth's surface, atmosphere and astronomical observations are mainly collected through scientific satellites. Weather satellites broadcast photographs and information related to cloud patterns and measure other meteorological conditions that help predict the weather. Relays made by communications satellites enable us to receive and make phone calls, receive radio and television programmes and also access the internet from different parts of the planet. Some satellites help in navigation to determine the position of ships and airplanes. The **Global Positioning System (GPS)** also uses navigation satellites. It is a space-based radio-navigation system that helps us find our location regardless of where we are in the world. Military satellites carry out military observation and surveillance.

▶ Many cars and phones today have GPS navigation systems that help people find their destinations

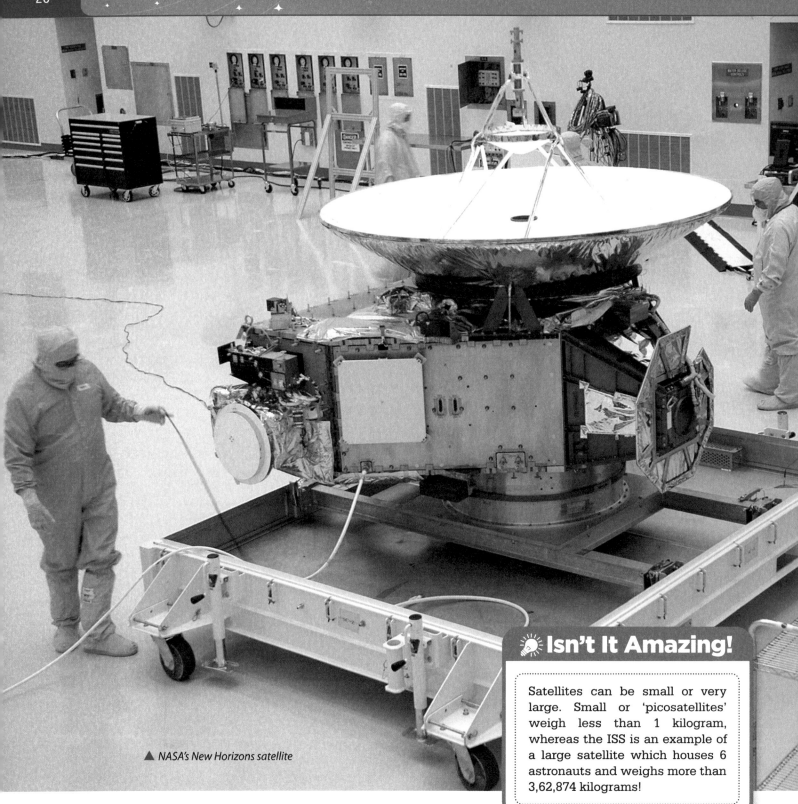

▲ *NASA's New Horizons satellite*

⭐ How Do Satellites Work?

Depending on the mission of a satellite, the technology on-board will vary. Computers aboard the satellite not only help receive and store data but also transmit information in the form of radio signals back to stations on Earth. When scientists receive this information, they analyse the data and understand its implications. One method to do this is by feeding this data into computer models that use **algorithms** or mathematical formulas. The data is used by researchers to virtually recreate the processes that are happening on Earth, for example, how the atmosphere, water bodies and land surfaces interrelate as a system. These computerised simulations enable an understanding of the correlation between Earth's systems and how its environment will change in the future. The high-resolution images of Pluto's icy surface sent back to Earth by NASA's New Horizons spacecraft is just one such example of the exemplary work done by artificial satellites.

Small Satellites

Artificial satellites vary in size and cost. They can be small enough to fit in the palm, or as large as the International Space Station. Small satellites can be further classified on the basis of their weight into minisatellites, microsatellites, nanosatellites, picosatellites and femtosatellites. These are used in many space applications.

▲ *An astronomer holds up a KickSat, a femtosatellite*

Generic Name	Launch Weight
Minisatellite	100–180 kg
Microsatellite	10–100 kg
Nanosatellite	1–10 kg
Picosatellite	0.01–1 kg
Femtosatellite	0.001–0.01 kg

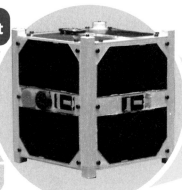

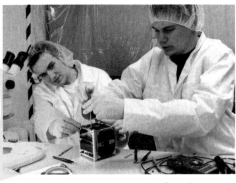

▲ *ESTCube-1 is an example of a CubeSat*

⭐ Challenges to Small Satellites

There is uncertainty in the sustainability of the business of small companies which make small satellites. They use multiple small satellites to deliver global high-resolution photos of Earth, daily. These are used for a wide range of important services such as gauging agricultural yield, oil and natural gas exploration and production, deforestation, mapping and geospatial services, tracking of ships in seas, emergency response, national security, mobile device support, etc.

There is limited availability of adequate radio spectrum. Frequencies for CubeSats (a class of nanosatellites) are in the UHF band (435–438 MHz). They are governed by the International Amateur Radio Union (IARU). These bandwidths are small and can transmit only limited data. Higher frequency bands yield wider bandwidths but need a special license.

▲ *Three microsatellites placed together*

Small satellite companies must also behave responsibly and pay great attention to the challenge of clean-up and removal of orbital debris (also known as space debris or space junk), which refers to stray man-made objects floating in space. It can travel at speeds up to eight kilometres per second. At such high speeds, even a fleck of paint can damage spacecrafts. Unfortunately, there are hundreds of thousands of such pieces floating in space. Small satellite makers will need to design new ways to deorbit after completing their missions, as the debris poses extreme danger to human life and property (such as the ISS) in space.

⭐ ISRO Nano Satellites

▲ *MAYA-1, a nanosatellite built in the Philippines*

ISRO (Indian Space Research Organisation) Nano Satellites (INS) is a nanosatellite bus system to carry experimental payloads (cargoes) up to 3 kilograms. The INS system accompanies bigger satellites on Polar Satellite Launch Vehicles (PLSV). The main goals are to conceptualise and make low-cost modular nanosatellites, carry ISRO technology payloads, provide a standard vehicle for on-demand services and carry materials for universities and research and development laboratories.

PSLV-C37 carried two ISRO Nano Satellites—INS-1A and INS-1B as co-passenger satellites, launched on February 15, 2017. INS-1C was launched by PSLV-C40 on Jan 12, 2018. Small satellites are continuously being made cheaper, faster and with less wastage by leveraging 3D printing technology.

Demystifying and Calculating Distances in Space

How do scientists measure astronomical distances of celestial objects and find out how far they are? On Earth, we measure 'distance' in kilometres or miles. Similarly, distances of objects in space have specific measurements and units.

⭐ Light year and Astronomical Unit

In astronomy, vast distances in space are calculated using the unit of **light year**, which is the distance travelled by light (moving in a vacuum) in one year, at 29,97,92,458 miles per second. An **Astronomical Unit (AU)** is a unit of measurement equal to 149.6 million kilometres, which is the mean distance between the centres of Earth and the Sun. So, one light year is equal to about 9.44 trillion kilometres or 63,241 AU.

Proxima Centauri is the star closest to Earth. It is 4.24 light years away from Earth and is a dwarf star. Even though it is the closest star, walking to Proxima Centauri would take 215 million years and travelling to it on the Apollo 11 spacecraft would still take 43,000 years! That is how far objects in space are. So, it is much easier to talk about their distances in light years, rather than referring to them in millions, billions or even trillions of kilometres or miles.

⭐ Measuring Distances

In astronomy, geometry is used to measure distances between celestial bodies like a planet and a star or two stars. One of the most accurate methods used to measure distances to stars is called '**parallax**', and its unit is an **arcsecond**. But what exactly are these two units?

▼ An illustration of a space satellite orbiting Earth

⭕ Incredible Individuals

One of the most important American astronomers in the first half of the 20th century was Henry Norris Russell (1877–1957). He played a key role in laying the foundations of modern theoretical astrophysics by making physics the central subject in astrophysical practice.

▲ American astronomer Henry Norris Russell spent most of his professional life at Princeton University as a student, instructor and professor and later as director of the observatory

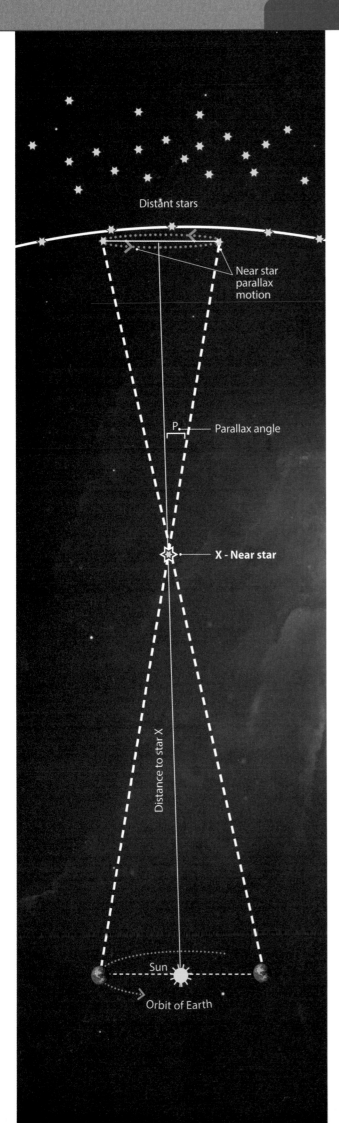

Distant stars

Near star parallax motion

P. — Parallax angle

X - Near star

Distance to star X

Sun

Orbit of Earth

 # Understanding Parallax

A parallax is the difference in direction of a celestial object, as seen by an observer from two widely separated points. Try this experiment to understand what a parallax is:

- raise a finger in front of your face at an arm's distance. Keep still and be careful not to move your finger.

- close one eye and observe the position of your finger with the other eye.

- now, close that eye and open the other. Observe the position of your finger again. What did you notice?

It would appear that the position of your finger has 'shifted' a small distance in relation to the more distant objects behind it. Your finger and your two eyes are three points on a plane that form a long triangle. The shift that you notice is caused due to your eyes being separated from each other by a few inches. So, each eye sees the finger in front of you from a slightly different angle. That small angle by which your finger appears to move is known as the parallax.

Now, instead of your two eyes, take the base of the triangle as the two points on Earth that are on opposite sides of the Sun. The star marked as X in the diagram is like your finger. The line shown going up from the Sun to star X (seen in the middle of the diagram) is the distance between the Sun and star X. If you click a photograph of a star, it will seemingly move relative to the background stars, just like your hand seemingly shifted relative to your surroundings. Knowing the parallax angle that the star moved and the size of Earth's orbit, one can calculate the distance to the star.

◀ *A stellar parallax diagram*

 # Arcseconds and Parsecs

Since the parallax angle by which even the nearest stars appear to have moved is so small, it is difficult to measure this distance. Parallax is measured using a unit called an arcsecond. A circle has 360 degrees. Each degree is the same as 60 arcminutes. 1 arcminute is the same as 60 arcseconds. So, 1 arcsecond is 1/3600th of a degree. Usually, a unit called **parsec** is used to measure interstellar distances. A parsec is the distance at which a star has a parallax of 1 arcsecond. 1 parsec is the same as 3.26 light years or 2,06,000 AU. Parsec is used to measure larger distances, while parallax or arcsecond is used to measure smaller distances.

The Future of Space Exploration

Over the years, humans have made incredible progress in space exploration. The 21st century is also called the Age of Information and Technology. The study of space has become even more exciting in this century, thanks to innovations in space travel and exploration.

▲ The Orion space capsule and the ISS photographed in September 2006

⭐ Recent Developments

NASA recently launched its new-generation Orion spacecraft and will soon complete building the massive tennis-court sized James Webb Space Telescope. ESA successfully landed a space probe called Rosetta on a comet, 510 million kilometres away. China has begun developing its next space station. India is preparing for its first manned mission to space to be carried out by 2022!

There are many other new developments in the field of space exploration. Low-cost recyclable rockets could be a possibility in the future. People might be able to take short space vacations of 7–10 minutes. Some astronomers even believe that human beings could form a colony on planet Mars, though this might only be possible in the distant future.

▲ NASA's James Webb Space Telescope is a marvellous engineering accomplishment and is the most advanced space observatory in the world

⭐ Private Spaceflights

Private companies have played a part in spaceflights since 1962, when NASA launched its first privately-made satellite. Today, companies like SpaceX and Boeing have started competing for big government contracts.

On February 6, 2018, SpaceX successfully launched an operational rocket named Falcon Heavy into space. It carried a Tesla Roadster, which is an electric sports car. Starman, a mannequin dressed in a spacesuit, sat in the driver's seat of the car. Falcon Heavy became the most powerful operational launch vehicle in the world.

Blue Origin and Virgin Galactic are some other examples of private companies that have ventured into space tourism. Blue Origin's upgraded New Shepard spacecraft shows amazing views of Earth. It went on its tenth test flight in January 2019. This marks another step towards sending paying tourists into suborbital space.

◀ Launched by SpaceX, Falcon Heavy's side boosters land on Landing Zone 1 (LZ1) and Landing Zone 2 (LZ2) during a demo mission

▲ *An astronaut exploring the lunar surface*

 # Headed to the Moon

To explore distant worlds, Moon missions are essential. Long-duration visits to Earth's satellite help build the experience and expertise required for similar long-term space expeditions to other planets. The Moon can also be used as an operational base where astronauts can restock supplies (including rocket fuel and oxygen) by making them from local materials. Even though people have been to the Moon before, there are still many things left to be explored. For example, astronomers and scientists need to visit the Moon's poles to investigate if water, in the form of ice, exists there. Future missions to the Moon are certainly on the cards.

▲ *A mock-up of the Orion spacecraft at the Johnson Space Center demonstrates how crew members would be seated during a launch*

▲ *Technicians carrying out some work on the Orion crew module at NASA's John F Kennedy Space Center in Florida*

In Real Life

The Falcon Heavy launch generated excitement amongst the general public and space industry. Along with broadcasts of Starman, the launch was viewed 40 million times on SpaceX's YouTube channel. The company has since then bagged its first competitive contract from the US Air Force.

▲ *Maiden launch of SpaceX's Falcon Heavy*

State-of-the-art Spacecrafts

The new NASA missions are getting more advanced with state-of-the-art technologies. For example, the design of NASA's Orion crew exploration vehicle is along the lines of the earlier Apollo missions, but with upgraded systems that use modern technology. The new capsules will be large enough to accommodate four crew members and have three times the volume capacity. The Orion capsules are supposed to be safer and more reliable than the space shuttle.

An added innovation is that they are built to be reused up to ten and will use the same method of parachuting back to Earth, but will land on dry land, instead of an ocean splashdown. Having launched Orion in an unmanned test flight in December 2014, NASA aims to send a crewed mission on it in 2020. Such new-age space vehicles herald a new period in space exploration—one which will take human beings farther than they have ever been before, including in close proximity to the Moon and Mars!

Space Tourism

Recreational space travel is known as space tourism. Presently, space tourists can visit celestial bodies on government-owned spacecrafts like the Soyuz and the ISS. While it is not very common, people might also be able to travel to space on vehicles operated by private companies.

▲ *Dennis Tito (extreme left)— the first American space-flight participant—along with a Soyuz commander and flight engineer. The trio took off from the Baikonur Cosmodrome in Kazakhstan*

⭐ Orbital versus Suborbital Flights

Would you like to zoom off into space and go where no private citizen could have gone prior to 2001? Now you can! In fact, you can choose between an orbital space flight and a suborbital flight. There is an astronomical difference in the cost that may help you make your decision.

The difference between an orbital and suborbital flight is in its trajectory. A trajectory is the path that a rocket or spacecraft takes. An orbital flight continuously goes around Earth, moving very fast. A suborbital flight entails lift-off, making a great arc and falling back to reach Earth. Going into space is expensive. An orbital space tourism flight would be more expensive, since the spacecraft has to reach a speed of almost 12,874 kmps to get into orbit. However, going into space and falling back to Earth would use less energy and is therefore less expensive.

Orbital space tourism flights began with an American businessman named Dennis Tito in April 2001. He paid $20 million for a flight aboard the Soyuz TM-32, which took him to the ISS. He spent seven days at the ISS. Several other individuals from different countries went on space tourism flights thereafter. A company called Space Adventures even offered a spaceflight around the Moon on a Soyuz craft for an amount of $100 million!

💡 Isn't It Amazing!

XCOR's EZ-Rocket, a ground-launched, rocket-powered aircraft piloted by Dick Rutan created history, in 2005, with its record-setting point-to-point flight from the Mojave California Spaceport.

▶ *XCOR Aerospace's EZ-Rocket landing in California city*

▼ *Virgin Galactica 1*

▲ *The Soyuz TM-32 can be seen here after leaving from the ISS*

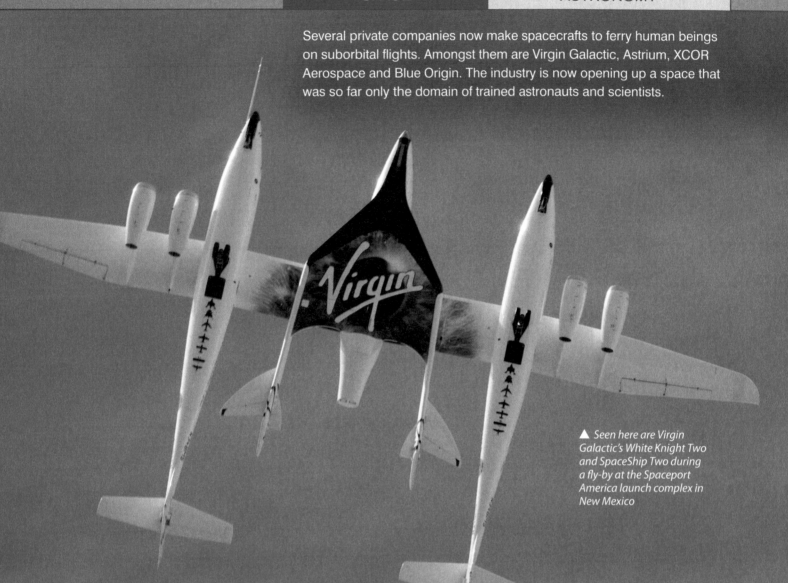

Several private companies now make spacecrafts to ferry human beings on suborbital flights. Amongst them are Virgin Galactic, Astrium, XCOR Aerospace and Blue Origin. The industry is now opening up a space that was so far only the domain of trained astronauts and scientists.

▲ *Seen here are Virgin Galactic's White Knight Two and SpaceShip Two during a fly-by at the Spaceport America launch complex in New Mexico*

 ## Why is Space Tourism Significant?

Notwithstanding the prohibitive costs there are benefits of space tourism, which some people feel will eventually help the entire human race.

The space tourism industry now has private players, so space ambitions and missions will no longer be dependent on government funding. Commercial spaceflight companies are already researching capsules to take tourists around the Moon and even land on Mars. This will create and motivate a new generation of engineers who will get an opportunity to be at the forefront of space exploration.

With increased competition, the cost of reaching space is likely to reduce. Currently, private space companies are in the early stages of developing first-generation rocket planes. Eventually, suborbital, point-to-point flights may become a reality and transport people at a fraction of the time it currently takes. Suborbital flights will cater not only to space tourism but also to scientific research. This could also have environmental benefits.

When astronauts first viewed Earth from space as a tiny round blue speck against the vastness of the universe, it changed their view of our planet. That's another reason why space tourism is significant. Space travel will change our perspective and world view for the better and help us strive harder to solve some of Earth's biggest problems like climate change, pollution, etc.

▲ *A view of the mock-up interior of the European Aeronautic Defence and Space Company Astrium Space Tourism Project*

Robotics

The design, construction and use of machines (robots) to do tasks which were conventionally done by human beings is termed robotics. Robots are often used in automobile manufacturing and in industries with hazardous environments. They are used to invent diagnostic and surgical techniques in the field of medicine. Some robots are equipped with **artificial intelligence (AI)**, which allows them to function in a way similar to humans. They might have vision, touch, temperature-sensing mechanisms and simple decision-making features. Some robots are even shaped like human beings. They are called androids. Today's robots have come a long way from the first one installed in 1961 in a factory by General Motors, which was used to move hot metal pieces.

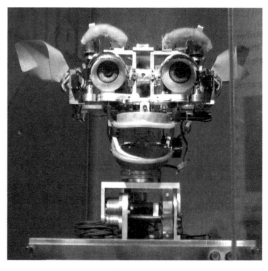

▲ *Kismet is a robot that was programmed with some social skills. Replicating social skills has been a challenging task in robotics*

What do Robots do in Space?

One big advantage of sending robots into space is that we need not worry too much about their safety, unlike in the case of human astronauts. Scientists certainly need these well-crafted robots to last for a long time to investigate, conduct experiments and send back data and information about their destinations. But sending robots helps save human lives, in case there is a mishap or the mission fails.

It is also less expensive to send a robot to space. Robots do not eat, sleep or go to the washroom. They can survive in outer space for many years. Some are even left there with no need for a return journey.

▶ *NASA's Mars Exploration Rover is seen on the surface of Mars. The first two rovers were launched within weeks of each other. They were the rovers Opportunity and Spirit*

Another advantage of doing so is that robots can undertake risky tasks that humans cannot. They can bear harsh conditions in space, like very low or high temperatures and increased levels of radiation. Therefore, advances in robotics have also expanded the scope of space exploration.

▲ This self-portrait of the Curiosity rover was taken at one of its first drill sites

⭐ NASA's Robots

Curiosity, Spirit and Opportunity are among the most well-known and popular rovers built by NASA to investigate Mars.

NASA's more recent robots are Puffer (Pop-Up Flat Folding Explorer Rover) and BRUIE (the Buoyant Rover for Under-Ice Exploration). Origami designs have been the inspiration behind Puffer, which is a very lightweight, two-wheeled robot that can make itself flat and crouch down to explore tight spots.

BRUIE is unique as it can float on water, take photographs, collect data and travel with ease on the bottom of an icy surface using wheels.

Sometime in the future, it may be possible for robots like these to look for signs of life on icy bodies in the solar system.

▶ A computer-aided-design drawing of NASA's 2020 Mars rover

⭐ Other Types of Robots

Not all robots are rovers, some take on other curious shapes, like the Hedgehog, which is a spiky, cube-shaped robot being built by NASA along with Stanford University and Massachusetts Institute of Technology (MIT), USA. The Hedgehog robot is mainly being designed to explore asteroids or comets which are smaller celestial bodies that have very little gravity and an uneven terrain. So, instead of rolling on four wheels like a rover, this one hops and tumbles and can operate on any one of its sides.

R5 or Valkyrie developed by NASA's Johnson Space Center is a humanoid robot. These robots are made because there are some situations where it is best for a robot to have human-like movements to carry out particular tasks. For example, similar robots could be useful in helping human beings settle on Mars in the future. Irrespective of their shape, size and function, robots are an important invention for space exploration.

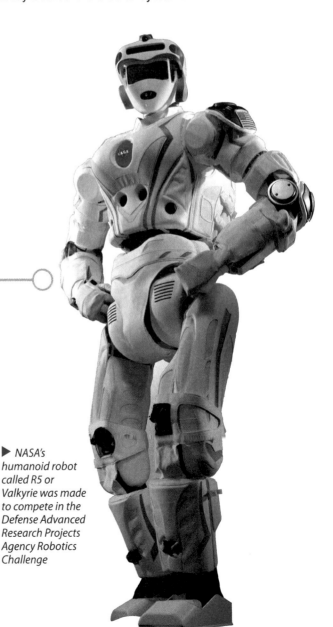

▶ NASA's humanoid robot called R5 or Valkyrie was made to compete in the Defense Advanced Research Projects Agency Robotics Challenge

Future Space Missions

"To confine our attention to terrestrial matters would be to limit the human spirit."
— Stephen Hawking

The human spirit has always sought a challenge. Space exploration is one such challenging area. As long as the universe exists, scientists will continue to seek answers about its origins by employing advanced technology, instruments, satellites and space probes. Scientific inquiry, rivalry and competition amongst nations, commercial gains, and the search for 'other habitable' planets are the other motivations that have led to advancements in space exploration.

 ## Future Space Missions

The 2020 Mars Rover

Camera technology has greatly advanced since NASA's Mars Pathfinder, with five cameras, landed in 1997. The 2020 rover Perseverance will have 23 cameras. It will explore a region of the planet believed to have supported microbial life many years ago. The rover will also perform an experiment to extract oxygen from the Martian atmosphere, provide landscape photographs, reveal obstacles and study the atmosphere.

▲ *A computer-assisted-design work of NASA's 2020 Mars rover Perseverance*

Lunar Flashlight

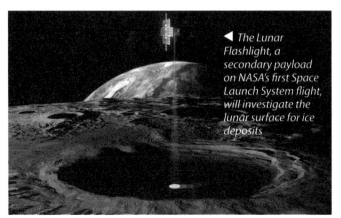

◄ *The Lunar Flashlight, a secondary payload on NASA's first Space Launch System flight, will investigate the lunar surface for ice deposits*

NASA's Lunar Flashlight (planned launch in 2020) on the Space Launch System's Exploration Mission-1 (EM-1) flight will map the Moon's south pole for volatiles (components that are gases at room temperature) and will be the first CubeSat to reach the Moon, use green propulsion and look for water ice using lasers.

Mid-Infrared Instrument (MIRI)

MIRI will play a crucial role in NASA's James Webb Space Telescope and will click images of stars and galaxies in infrared light. The data generated will throw light on the evolution of the universe and the search for the very first star formation episode.

▲ *(L-R): Pictures of the Mid-Infrared Instrument (MIRI) and a NASA engineer inspecting copper test wires inside the thermal shield of MIRI which will travel aboard the James Webb Space Telescope*

▲ *An artist's rendering of the Europa Clipper spacecraft, as per NASA's Jet Propulsion Lab*

NASA's Mission to Europa

NASA's Europa Clipper, a radiation-tolerant spacecraft with nine scientific instruments on-board, will study Europa (one of Jupiter's largest moons) to search for conditions that may support life. There has been some proof that an ocean of liquid water exists below the icy moon's crust. It will do a long, looping orbit around Jupiter with a series of close fly-bys of Europa.

▲ *Developed by NASA, the DSAC, a miniature mercury-ion atomic clock is expected to improve the precision of navigation in deep space*

NASA's Deep Space Atomic Clock (DSAC)

DSAC is 50 times more accurate than the best navigation clocks today. It is a small, ultra-precise mercury-ion atomic clock to be used for radio navigation, i.e. using radio frequencies to accurately determine the position of something. Radio navigation is vital for deep-space exploration missions. The DSAC will improve navigation of spacecrafts to reach far-off places, enable gathering of more data with enhanced precision, and help in radio science and GPS.

INSPIRE

NASA's Interplanetary NanoSpacecraft Pathfinder In Relevant Environment (INSPIRE) mission plans to show the groundbreaking capability of deep-space CubeSats by putting a nano spacecraft in Earth-escape orbit.

▼ *The ESA's mission, Euclid will map the geometry of the dark universe*

⭐ The Euclid Mission

Euclid is a planned mission of the ESA with significant inputs from NASA. These inputs include infrared detectors for one instrument and science and data analysis. The mission plans to investigate and provide information on dark matter and dark energy. The scheduled launch is in 2020.

⭐ Gaganyaan

One of India's most ambitious space projects is Gaganyaan. ISRO's Human Space Flight Centre is responsible for its implementation. It will be India's first manned mission and will take three Indian astronauts into space for seven days in low-Earth orbit. The mission will make India only the fourth country in the world after the USA, Russia and China to send human beings to space!

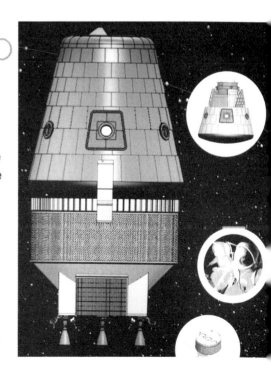

▶ *An info-graphic displayed at the Bangalore Space Expo (September 2018), shows ISRO's Gaganyaan orbital vehicle's Crew and Service Module*

Word Check

Algorithm: It is a systematic procedure that produces—in a finite number of steps—the answer to a question or the solution of a problem.

Arcsecond: It is 1/3600th of a degree and the unit to measure parallax.

Artificial Intelligence (AI): It means making machines that can reason, take decisions which usually require human expertise, and carry out human-like tasks.

Astrology: It is a type of divination that involves the forecasting of earthly and human events through the observation and interpretation of the movement of the stars, the Sun, the Moon and the planets. It has no basis in science.

Astronomical Unit (AU): It is a unit of measurement equal to 149.6 million kilometres, which is the mean distance from the centre of Earth to the centre of the Sun.

Astrophysics: It is a branch of astronomy concerned primarily with the properties and structure of cosmic objects, including the universe as a whole.

Biomass burning: It refers to the burning of living or dead vegetation including grassland, forest, agricultural waste, etc., for fuel. Burning can be natural (caused by lightning) or man-made (due to the burning of vegetation for land clearing, fuelwood, etc.)

Diffraction: It is the phenomenon of light bending when it passes around an edge or through a slit.

Geocentric model: According to this theory, Earth lies at the centre of the solar system or universe. It has now been debunked.

Global Positioning System (GPS): It is a space-based radio-navigation system that broadcasts highly accurate navigation pulses to users on or near Earth.

Heliocentric model: According to this theory, the Sun is considered to be the central figure within the solar system, around which Earth and other planets revolve.

Light year: It is the distance travelled by light (moving in a vacuum) in one year, at 29,97,92,458 miles per second.

Oxidiser: A type of chemical (like oxygen) required for a fuel to burn

Parallax: It is the difference in direction of a celestial object as seen by an observer from two widely separated points.

Parsec: It is used to measure interstellar distances. A parsec is the distance at which a star has a parallax of 1 arcsecond.

Propellants: It is a substance that propels or pushes something forward.

Propulsion: It means producing a force that pushes or drives an object forward, like moving an aircraft forward through air.

Sextant: It is an instrument used to determine the angle between the horizon and a celestial object like a star, the Sun or the Moon.

Spectroscope: It is an instrument designed for visual observation of spectra. In optics, spectrum is the arrangement of visible, ultraviolet and infrared light according to their wavelength.

Trigonometry: It is a field of mathematics concerned with functions of angles and their application to calculations.